CANADI

G.O.A.T.

11 Greatest Canadians of All Time

DIPAN KUMAR DAS

SUDIP KUMAR DAS

This book is dedicated to all the people of Canada, past and present, whose collective contributions and diverse stories have shaped this nation into the remarkable place it is today. It is also dedicated to those who tirelessly work towards making Canada a better and more inclusive country for future generations.

In the spirit of the 11 remarkable Canadians highlighted in these pages, may we all find inspiration to strive for greatness, to stand up for justice, and to leave a positive legacy in our own unique ways. This dedication is a tribute to the shared values of unity, diversity, and progress that define Canada.

Foreword

In the pages that follow, we embark on a journey through the lives and legacies of 11 exceptional Canadians, each a true "G.O.A.T." (Greatest of All Time) in their own right. Canada, a nation known for its vast landscapes and rich cultural tapestry, has produced individuals whose impact extends far beyond its borders.

As we delve into the stories of Sir John A. Macdonald, Terry Fox, Tommy Douglas, Lester B. Pearson, Pierre Elliott Trudeau, Emily Carr, Viola Desmond, David Suzuki, Wayne Gretzky, Margaret Atwood, and Louis Riel, we encounter a diverse array of talents and achievements. From politics to art, sports to social justice, and environmental advocacy to literature, these remarkable Canadians have left their mark on the world.

Each of these individuals represents a unique chapter in Canada's history, reflecting the values, challenges, and aspirations of the nation. Their stories inspire us to recognize the potential for greatness within ourselves and to embrace the values of compassion, inclusivity, and resilience that define Canada.

As we journey through these pages, may we celebrate the achievements of these 11 iconic figures and, in doing so, find inspiration to contribute to the ongoing narrative of Canada's greatness. For Canada is a nation of diverse voices, each capable of making a profound difference in the world.

This book serves as a tribute to the spirit of Canada and its people, past and present. May their stories inspire us to reach for new heights, break down barriers, and leave a lasting, positive impact on our communities and the world at large.

Let us now turn the page and begin this exploration of the 11 Greatest Canadians of All Time.

Preface

In the vibrant tapestry of history, there are moments and individuals that stand out, forever etching their legacies into the collective memory of a nation. Canada, a land of breathtaking landscapes and diverse cultures, has been home to countless such moments and individuals who have left an indelible mark on its story.

In the pages that follow, we embark on a journey to discover the lives and achievements of 11 remarkable Canadians, each celebrated as a "G.O.A.T." - the Greatest of All Time - in their respective fields. From pioneering politicians to tireless activists, visionary artists to legendary athletes, these individuals have enriched Canada's cultural fabric and contributed to its global standing.

Through their stories, we gain insight into the forces that have shaped Canada, from its early days of Confederation to its present as a dynamic and inclusive nation. We explore the struggles and triumphs, the passions and perseverance that have defined these 11 lives and the impact they've had on the world.

As we delve into the stories of Sir John A. Macdonald, Terry Fox, Tommy Douglas, Lester B. Pearson, Pierre Elliott Trudeau, Emily Carr, Viola Desmond, David Suzuki, Wayne Gretzky, Margaret Atwood, and Louis Riel, we aim to celebrate not only their individual greatness but also the shared values they represent: equality, justice, innovation, and a profound connection to the Canadian spirit.

This book is a tribute to Canada and its people, a nation known for its resilience, its reverence for nature, its commitment to multiculturalism, and its dedication to making the world a better place. It is an exploration of the diverse paths that have led these 11 individuals to greatness and a reflection on the impact they continue to have on Canada and the global stage.

As we delve into their lives, may we find inspiration in their journeys, their challenges, and their unwavering dedication to their respective callings. In celebrating the achievements of these remarkable Canadians, we celebrate Canada itself and the enduring values that define this extraordinary nation.

Join us as we embark on a journey through history, culture, and the essence of Canada's greatness, one captivating story at a time.

Prologue

In the vast expanse of Canada, a land as diverse as it is beautiful, there exists a rich tapestry of stories that have shaped the nation's identity.

From coast to coast, from the northern tundra to the southern forests, these stories have been woven by individuals who have left an indelible mark on the country's history, culture, and spirit.

In the pages that follow, we delve into the lives of 11 extraordinary Canadians, each celebrated as a "G.O.A.T." – the Greatest of All Time – in their own unique way. These remarkable individuals represent a cross-section of Canada's greatness, their achievements spanning the realms of politics, sports, art, literature, social justice, and environmental advocacy.

As we journey through the stories of Sir John A. Macdonald, Terry Fox,

Tommy Douglas, Lester B. Pearson, Pierre Elliott Trudeau, Emily Carr, Viola Desmond, David Suzuki, Wayne Gretzky, Margaret Atwood, and Louis Riel, we come to understand the diverse forces and passions that have defined Canada. From the early days of Confederation to the present, these lives have intersected with pivotal moments in the nation's evolution.

But this is not just a collection of biographies; it is a celebration of Canada's spirit. It is an exploration of the values that have made Canada a beacon of hope, tolerance, and innovation on the global stage. It is a tribute to the determination, compassion, and creativity that course through the veins of this extraordinary nation.

As we embark on this journey, may we find inspiration in the stories of these remarkable Canadians, who have not only achieved greatness but have also enriched the nation's cultural heritage and contributed to the betterment of the world. Their lives serve as a testament to the enduring values of equality, justice, and the pursuit of excellence that define the Canadian identity.

Join us as we embark on this voyage through Canada's past and present, guided by the stories of 11 exceptional individuals who embody the spirit of the Great White North. In celebrating their achievements, we

celebrate Canada itself and the
promise of a brighter future.

CHAPTER ONE

Sir John A. Macdonald

Sir John A. Macdonald, full name Sir John Alexander Macdonald, was a prominent Canadian statesman and the first Prime Minister of Canada. He was born on January 11, 1815, in Glasgow, Scotland, and passed away on June 6, 1891, in Ottawa, Ontario. Here is a brief overview of his life and contributions:

Early Life:

Macdonald immigrated to Kingston, Ontario, with his family at the age of five.

He pursued a legal career and established a successful law practice in Kingston.

Political Career:

Macdonald entered politics in the 1840s and quickly rose through the ranks.

He was a key figure in the discussions leading to the Confederation of Canada in 1867.

Macdonald became Canada's first Prime Minister in 1867 and served for 19 years in total, making him one of the longest-serving prime ministers in Canadian history.

As Prime Minister, he played a crucial role in uniting the provinces into the Dominion of Canada and expanding its territory through initiatives like the Canadian Pacific Railway.

Macdonald's National Policy promoted economic growth by implementing protective tariffs and supporting western expansion.

Legacy:

He is often referred to as the "Father of Confederation" for his pivotal role in shaping the Canadian Confederation.

Macdonald's leadership helped Canada overcome many early challenges, including securing a transcontinental railway, maintaining political stability, and fostering national identity.

Despite his contributions, Macdonald's legacy is also marked by controversy, notably his government's policies towards Indigenous peoples, including the residential school system.

His image is featured on the Canadian ten-dollar bill, and numerous landmarks, streets, and institutions bear his name.

Sir John A. Macdonald remains a central figure in Canadian history, revered for his role in establishing the foundation of modern Canada, even as his legacy continues to be debated and scrutinized in light of changing historical perspectives.

CHAPTER TWO
Terry Fox

Terry Fox was a courageous and inspirational Canadian athlete and humanitarian known for his remarkable Marathon of Hope. Born on July 28, 1958, in Winnipeg, Manitoba, and passing away on June 28, 1981, in New Westminster, British Columbia, here is an overview of his remarkable life and legacy:

Early Life:

Terry Fox grew up in Port Coquitlam, British Columbia, as an active and sports-loving child.

In 1977, at the age of 18, he was diagnosed with bone cancer (osteosarcoma), which resulted in the amputation of his right leg above the knee.

The Marathon of Hope:

In 1980, inspired by the suffering of cancer patients and determined to raise awareness and funds for cancer research, Terry Fox embarked on the "Marathon of Hope."

He began his run on April 12, 1980, in St. John's, Newfoundland, with the goal of running across Canada, covering over 5,000 kilometers (3,100 miles).

Running approximately a marathon's distance (26 miles) every day on his prosthetic leg, Fox became a symbol of determination and hope for millions of Canadians.

His journey captured the nation's attention, and he received widespread support and donations for cancer research.

Unfortunately, after 143 days and over 3,000 kilometers (1,900 miles) into his run, Terry Fox was forced to stop near Thunder Bay, Ontario, when his cancer had spread to his lungs.

Legacy:

Terry Fox's Marathon of Hope raised over $24 million for cancer research in Canada during his lifetime.

He became a national hero and an international symbol of resilience, courage, and hope.

The annual Terry Fox Run, held in his memory, is one of the world's largest one-day fundraising events for cancer research, and it takes place in numerous countries.

The Terry Fox Foundation continues to raise funds for cancer research, and the Terry Fox Research Institute is dedicated to finding ways to prevent, detect, and treat cancer.

Terry Fox's story has been immortalized in books, documentaries, films, and statues across Canada.

Terry Fox's indomitable spirit and unwavering commitment to making a difference in the fight against cancer continue to inspire people around the world. His legacy lives on through the ongoing efforts to find a cure for cancer and the annual Terry Fox Run, where millions of individuals come together to honor his memory and support cancer research.

CHAPTER THREE
Tommy Douglas

Tommy Douglas, whose full name was Thomas Clement Douglas, was a revered Canadian politician and a key figure in the development of Canada's healthcare system. Born on October 20, 1904, in Falkirk, Scotland, and passing away on February 24, 1986, in Ottawa,

Ontario, here's an overview of his life and contributions:

Early Life:

Tommy Douglas immigrated with his family to Winnipeg, Manitoba, in 1919, where he experienced firsthand the hardships faced by working-class families.

He attended Brandon College and later pursued a career in politics.

Political Career:

Douglas entered politics in the 1930s and became a prominent member of the Cooperative Commonwealth Federation (CCF), a socialist political party.

He was elected as a Member of Parliament in 1935 and served in both federal and provincial roles.

As Premier of Saskatchewan from 1944 to 1961, Douglas implemented groundbreaking social and economic reforms, including the introduction of universal healthcare.

Universal Healthcare:

Tommy Douglas is often referred to as the "Father of Medicare" for his pivotal role in the creation of Canada's publicly-funded healthcare system.

In 1962, Saskatchewan became the first province to introduce universal healthcare, providing medical services to all residents regardless of their ability to pay.

Douglas's advocacy for healthcare reform paved the way for the establishment of the national healthcare system that Canada enjoys today.

Legacy:

Douglas's tireless efforts to improve the lives of ordinary Canadians through social programs, including healthcare and pensions, have left an enduring mark on Canadian society.

He received numerous honors during his lifetime, including being named "The Greatest Canadian" in a national television contest in 2004.

The Tommy Douglas Secondary School in Vaughan, Ontario, and the Tommy Douglas Collegiate in Saskatoon, Saskatchewan, are named in his honor.

His daughter, Shirley Douglas, also became a prominent actress and social activist.

Tommy Douglas's dedication to social justice and his role in bringing universal healthcare to Canada have made him a beloved and influential figure in Canadian history. His vision and commitment to equitable access to healthcare continue to shape the nation's values and policies.

CHAPTER FOUR

Lester B. Pearson

Lester Bowles Pearson, often referred to as "Mike," was a highly influential Canadian statesman and diplomat who played a significant role in shaping Canada's international and domestic policies. Born on April 23, 1897, in Newtonbrook, Ontario, and passing away on December 27, 1972, in Ottawa, here's an overview of his life and contributions:

Early Life:

Lester Pearson served as a pilot in the Royal Flying Corps during World War I and later studied history at the University of Toronto.

He pursued postgraduate studies at Oxford University as a Rhodes Scholar.

Diplomatic Career:

Pearson joined the Canadian Department of External Affairs (now Global Affairs Canada) in 1928 and quickly rose through the diplomatic ranks.

He played a crucial role in Canada's response to the Suez Crisis of 1956, where he proposed the concept of United Nations peacekeeping forces, which earned him international acclaim.

Prime Ministership:

Lester Pearson became the 14th Prime Minister of Canada, serving from 1963 to 1968 as the leader of the Liberal Party.

His government introduced numerous significant policies and initiatives, including the creation of the Canada Pension Plan (CPP) and the establishment of a new Canadian flag, the Maple Leaf, in 1965.

Pearson's administration also implemented a universal healthcare system and promoted bilingualism in the federal government.

Nobel Peace Prize:

In 1957, Lester Pearson was awarded the Nobel Peace Prize for his pivotal role in resolving the Suez Crisis through peacekeeping efforts.

His proposal for the establishment of UN peacekeeping forces fundamentally changed the way international conflicts were addressed.

Legacy:

Lester B. Pearson is often celebrated for his diplomacy, commitment to peace, and efforts to shape Canada's social and cultural identity.

The Pearson International Airport in Toronto is named in his honor.

The Lester B. Pearson Award, now known as the NHL's Ted Lindsay Award, is given annually to the most outstanding player in the NHL, as voted by fellow players.

Lester B. Pearson's contributions to Canada's domestic policies and his international efforts in diplomacy and peacekeeping have solidified his status as one of Canada's most respected leaders. His legacy lives on not only through various awards and institutions bearing his name but also through the enduring values he promoted in Canadian society and on the global stage.

CHAPTER FIVE
Pierre Elliott Trudeau

Pierre Elliott Trudeau was a charismatic and influential Canadian politician who served as the 15th

Prime Minister of Canada. Born on October 18, 1919, in Montreal, Quebec, and passing away on September 28, 2000, in Montreal, here is an overview of his life and contributions:

Early Life:

Trudeau was raised in a bilingual and affluent family in Quebec.

He pursued higher education at several prestigious institutions, including Harvard University and the London School of Economics.

Entry into Politics:

Pierre Trudeau entered politics during a period of political and social upheaval in Canada in the 1960s.

He joined the Liberal Party of Canada and quickly gained prominence for his charismatic and dynamic leadership style.

Prime Ministership:

Trudeau became Canada's Prime Minister in 1968 and held the position until 1979. He returned for a second term from 1980 to 1984.

During his tenure, Trudeau introduced several landmark policies and initiatives, including the official recognition of bilingualism and multiculturalism.

He played a key role in the patriation of the Canadian Constitution from the United Kingdom in 1982, which included the adoption of the

Canadian Charter of Rights and Freedoms.

Trudeau's government implemented wage and price controls, pursued a policy of détente with the Soviet Union, and navigated Canada through significant constitutional challenges.

Legacy:

Pierre Trudeau is often regarded as one of the most transformative leaders in Canadian history.

His dedication to civil liberties, individual rights, and multiculturalism has left a lasting impact on Canadian society.

Trudeau's vision of a strong and united Canada, which accommodates its linguistic and cultural diversity, continues to influence the country's policies and values.

The Trudeau Airport in Montreal and the Trudeau Foundation, which supports research and leadership development, bear his name.

While Pierre Elliott Trudeau's leadership and policies generated both admiration and controversy, there is no doubt that he was a pivotal figure in Canada's history. His contributions to shaping modern Canada, particularly in the areas of constitutional reform and cultural pluralism, have left a profound and enduring legacy in the nation's political and social fabric.

CHAPTER SIX

Emily Carr

Emily Carr was a celebrated Canadian artist and writer known for her distinctive contributions to Canadian art and her portrayal of the Indigenous cultures and landscapes of the Pacific Northwest. Born on December 13, 1871, in Victoria, British Columbia, and passing away on March 2, 1945, in Victoria, here's an overview of her life and artistic legacy:

Early Life:

Emily Carr was raised in a conservative and affluent Victorian-era family.

She developed a deep affinity for nature and the indigenous cultures of British Columbia during her childhood, which later became central themes in her artwork.

Artistic Pursuits:

Carr initially trained as a traditional artist, studying in San Francisco and London.

She later adopted a more modern and expressive style, influenced by the Post-Impressionist and Fauvist movements.

Carr's art is known for its bold use of color, strong lines, and evocative depictions of the rugged landscapes of British Columbia.

Indigenous Culture and Influence:

Carr had a deep respect for and fascination with Indigenous cultures, particularly the First Nations peoples of the Pacific Northwest.

She made several trips to remote Indigenous villages and created numerous artworks depicting totem poles, masks, and other cultural elements.

Carr's work played a significant role in raising awareness about Indigenous cultures at a time when they were often misunderstood or ignored.

Recognition and Legacy:

Emily Carr faced challenges and adversity as a female artist in a predominantly male art world, but her perseverance and unique vision ultimately earned her recognition.

In the later years of her life, she gained national and international acclaim for her art.

Today, Carr is considered one of Canada's most celebrated and iconic artists, and her works are featured in major art galleries across the country.

The Emily Carr University of Art and Design in Vancouver, British Columbia, is named in her honor, and it continues to inspire and educate aspiring artists.

Emily Carr's legacy extends beyond her art; it encompasses her pioneering spirit, her role in promoting Indigenous cultures, and her lasting impact on Canadian art. Her work continues to captivate audiences and enrich Canada's cultural heritage, making her an enduring and revered figure in the country's artistic history.

CHAPTER SEVEN

Viola Desmond

Viola Desmond was a courageous Canadian civil rights activist who is best known for her stand against racial segregation in Nova Scotia, which has become a symbol of the struggle for racial equality in Canada. Born on July 6, 1914, in Halifax, Nova Scotia, and passing away on February 7, 1965, in New York City, here is an overview of her life and her significant contribution to the civil rights movement in Canada:

Early Life:

Viola Desmond was a Black woman who grew up in Halifax, Nova Scotia, during a time of systemic racism and segregation.

She trained as a beautician and eventually established her own beauty salon, the Desmond School of Beauty Culture, in Halifax.

The Incident:

On November 8, 1946, Viola Desmond made history when she went to a movie theater in New Glasgow, Nova Scotia, and refused to leave the whites-only section of the theater.

She had purchased a ticket for the balcony but chose to sit on the main floor, not realizing there was a segregation policy.

Viola's refusal to move resulted in her arrest, and she was subsequently charged with tax evasion for the price difference between the main floor and balcony tickets.

Legal Battle and Activism:

Viola Desmond's arrest and trial sparked a local civil rights movement and garnered national attention.

Although she lost her legal case, her actions raised awareness about racial segregation in Canada and the injustice she faced.

Her activism inspired future generations of Black Canadians to fight for civil rights and challenge racial discrimination.

Legacy:

Viola Desmond's story gained renewed attention in recent years, leading to widespread recognition of her courage and contributions to the civil rights movement.

In 2018, she became the first Canadian woman to appear alone on a regularly circulating banknote—the $10 bill.

The Viola Desmond Chair in Social Justice at Cape Breton University, among other honors, commemorates her legacy.

Viola Desmond's refusal to accept racial segregation and her willingness to take a stand against injustice have made her an enduring symbol of courage and resilience in the face of discrimination. Her legacy serves as a reminder of the ongoing struggle for equality and the importance of advocating for social justice in Canada and beyond.

CHAPTER EIGHT

David Suzuki

David Suzuki is a prominent Canadian scientist, environmentalist, broadcaster, and author who is known for his tireless efforts to raise awareness about environmental issues and promote sustainability. Born on March 24, 1936, in Vancouver, British Columbia, here is an overview of his life and his significant contributions to the environmental movement:

Early Life and Education:

David Suzuki grew up in Vancouver, surrounded by the natural beauty of British Columbia.

He earned a Ph.D. in zoology from the University of Chicago and went on to do research in genetics.

Broadcasting Career:

Suzuki began his career as a geneticist but soon transitioned to broadcasting.

He became a well-known television host, most notably for the long-running CBC television program "The Nature of Things," which has educated and inspired Canadians about environmental issues for decades.

Environmental Activism:

Suzuki is a passionate advocate for environmental conservation and sustainability.

He co-founded the David Suzuki Foundation in 1990, a nonprofit organization dedicated to addressing environmental challenges and promoting solutions.

Through his books, documentaries, and public speaking engagements, Suzuki has played a vital role in educating the public about climate change, biodiversity, and the importance of protecting the environment for future generations.

Awards and Recognition:

David Suzuki has received numerous awards and honors for his environmental work, including the Order of Canada and the United Nations Environment Program Medal.

He is widely regarded as one of the most influential environmentalists in the world.

Legacy:

Suzuki's impact on the environmental movement in Canada and globally is immeasurable.

He has helped shape public policy, influenced corporate practices, and inspired countless individuals to take action to protect the planet.

His emphasis on the interconnectedness of all life and the need for sustainable practices continues to resonate with people worldwide.

David Suzuki's dedication to environmental advocacy and his ability to communicate complex scientific concepts in an accessible way have made him a respected and influential figure in the quest for a more sustainable and ecologically responsible world. His work continues to inspire people to take action to protect the environment and address the urgent challenges of our time.

CHAPTER NINE

Wayne Gretzky

Wayne Gretzky, often referred to as "The Great One," is one of the most legendary and iconic figures in the history of ice hockey. Born on January 26, 1961, in Brantford, Ontario, Canada, Wayne Gretzky's remarkable career and contributions to the sport have left an indelible mark. Here's an overview of his life and his legendary status in the world of hockey:

Early Life and Early Hockey Career:

Wayne Gretzky displayed exceptional talent in hockey from a very young age.

He played in youth leagues in Brantford and quickly gained recognition for his scoring ability and playmaking skills.

Gretzky's prodigious talent led him to join the Sault Ste. Marie Greyhounds of the Ontario Hockey League (OHL) at the age of 16.

NHL Career:

In 1978, Wayne Gretzky entered the National Hockey League (NHL) as a member of the Edmonton Oilers.

He quickly established himself as a dominant force in the league, setting numerous scoring records and winning several league MVP awards.

Gretzky's time with the Oilers was marked by four Stanley Cup championships in the 1980s.

In 1988, he was traded to the Los Angeles Kings, where he continued to excel and popularize hockey in non-traditional markets like California.

Gretzky also played for the St. Louis Blues and the New York Rangers before retiring in 1999.

Career Achievements:

Wayne Gretzky's list of accomplishments is extensive and includes several NHL records that still stand, such as most career goals, assists, and points.

He won the Hart Trophy (NHL MVP) a record nine times.

Gretzky is a four-time Stanley Cup champion and a two-time Olympic gold medalist (1984 Canada Cup and 2002 Salt Lake City Olympics).

He was inducted into the Hockey Hall of Fame in 1999, immediately following his retirement.

Legacy:

Wayne Gretzky is often regarded as the greatest hockey player of all time, and his number 99 jersey is retired by the NHL, meaning no player can wear it league-wide.

His impact on the sport extends beyond the ice; he is credited with popularizing hockey in the United States and contributing to its growth worldwide.

Gretzky's influence on the game, his sportsmanship, and his humble demeanor have earned him the admiration of fans and fellow athletes alike.

Wayne Gretzky's legacy is not only defined by his extraordinary skills on the ice but also by his role as a global ambassador for the sport of hockey. He remains an enduring symbol of excellence and sportsmanship, inspiring generations of players and fans to appreciate the beauty and excitement of the game.

CHAPTER TEN
Margaret Atwood

Margaret Atwood is a highly acclaimed Canadian author known for her prolific literary career, which spans a wide range of genres and includes novels, poetry, essays, and literary criticism. Born on November 18, 1939, in Ottawa, Ontario, Canada, Margaret Atwood has made significant contributions to contemporary literature and is recognized for her thought-provoking and socially relevant works. Here is an overview of her life and her notable achievements:

Early Life and Education:

Margaret Atwood grew up in various parts of Canada, including Toronto and Ottawa.

She developed a love for literature and writing at an early age and began composing poetry during her teenage years.

Atwood attended the University of Toronto, where she studied English literature and graduated with a Bachelor of Arts degree in 1961.

Literary Career:

Margaret Atwood published her first book of poetry, "Double Persephone," in 1961.

She gained recognition as a poet in the 1960s and 1970s with works like

"The Circle Game" (1966) and "Power Politics" (1971).

Atwood's novels have received critical acclaim and have been translated into numerous languages. Notable novels include "The Handmaid's Tale" (1985), "Cat's Eye" (1988), "Alias Grace" (1996), and "The Blind Assassin" (2000).

"The Handmaid's Tale" is one of her most famous works and has been adapted into a successful television series.

Her writing often explores themes related to feminism, identity, power dynamics, and dystopian societies.

Awards and Honors:

Margaret Atwood has received numerous awards and honors throughout her career, including the Governor General's Award for Fiction in Canada and the Booker Prize for "The Blind Assassin" in 2000.

She was awarded the Golden Booker Prize in 2018 for her novel "The Handmaid's Tale," marking its enduring literary significance.

Atwood has been recognized with honorary degrees from several universities and has been inducted into various literary and cultural halls of fame.

Social and Environmental Activism:

In addition to her writing, Margaret Atwood is known for her activism in areas such as environmental conservation and human rights.

She has been a vocal advocate for climate change awareness and action.

Margaret Atwood's impact on contemporary literature is immense. Her works are celebrated for their insightful exploration of complex themes and their ability to provoke thought and discussion. As a writer and social commentator, Atwood continues to inspire readers and contribute to important dialogues on issues that shape society and humanity.

CHAPTER ELEVEN
Louis Riel

Louis Riel was a prominent Métis leader and a central figure in the history of Western Canada during the late 19th century. Born on October 22, 1844, in the Red River Settlement (now Winnipeg, Manitoba), and executed on November 16, 1885, in Regina, Saskatchewan, Riel's life and actions are often viewed through the lens of his role in advocating for the rights and autonomy of the Métis people. Here's an overview of his life and his significance in Canadian history:

Early Life:

Louis Riel was of Métis heritage, which is a distinct culture and community with both Indigenous and European ancestry.

He received an education in Montreal, Quebec, and became fluent in both English and French.

Riel's leadership qualities became evident during his early years as he worked to protect Métis land rights and their way of life.

The Red River Resistance:

Riel became a prominent figure during the Red River Resistance of 1869-1870, also known as the Red River Rebellion.

The resistance was sparked by the Canadian government's efforts to assert control over the Red River Settlement, which was predominantly Métis.

Riel emerged as the leader of the Métis, and under his guidance, they negotiated terms with the Canadian government through the Manitoba Act, which led to the creation of the Province of Manitoba in 1870.

Northwest Resistance:

In 1884, Louis Riel returned to the political stage as Métis communities in the Northwest faced land disputes, cultural pressures, and economic challenges.

Riel took a leadership role in what is now known as the Northwest

Resistance of 1885, or the North-West Rebellion.

The conflict between Métis and the Canadian government escalated into armed confrontations in areas like Duck Lake and Batoche, Saskatchewan.

Riel's leadership during this period was marked by a desire for justice and recognition of Métis rights.

Legacy:

Louis Riel's leadership, particularly during the Red River Resistance and the Northwest Resistance, has made him a symbol of Métis pride and the struggle for Indigenous rights and self-determination.

He remains a complex and polarizing figure in Canadian history, viewed by some as a hero and champion of Indigenous rights and by others as a rebel and a threat to Canadian sovereignty.

Riel's legacy continues to be a subject of debate and reflection in Canada.

Louis Riel's life and actions exemplify the ongoing struggle for Indigenous rights, autonomy, and recognition in Canada's history. His influence on Métis identity and the broader narrative of Indigenous rights in Canada is undeniable, making him a significant historical figure whose impact continues to be felt today.

Epilogue

In the epilogue of "Canadian G.O.A.T.: 11 Greatest Canadians of All Time," it is fitting to reflect on the enduring legacies of the remarkable individuals we've explored in this book. These 11 Canadians, each exceptional in their own way, have left an indelible mark on Canada's history, culture, and identity. Their stories serve as a testament to the diversity and richness of Canada's contributions to the world.

As we've journeyed through the lives of Sir John A. Macdonald, Terry Fox, Tommy Douglas, Lester B. Pearson, Pierre Elliott Trudeau, Emily Carr, Viola Desmond, David Suzuki, Wayne Gretzky, Margaret Atwood, and Louis Riel, we've encountered leaders in politics, sports, arts, social justice, and environmental advocacy. Their collective achievements have shaped Canada into the nation it is today.

These individuals remind us of the power of determination, innovation, and compassion. They have inspired generations and continue to do so, showing that great Canadians come from all walks of life and backgrounds. Their stories are a source of pride for all Canadians, as they reflect the values of equality, inclusivity, and respect that Canada aspires to uphold.

While these 11 figures have made significant contributions, let us not forget that there are countless other Canadians who have also played pivotal roles in their communities, the nation, and the world. Canada's strength lies in its diversity and the countless stories of individuals who have made a difference, both on a grand scale and in their everyday lives.

As we conclude this book, let it serve as a reminder that greatness is not limited to a select few. It is found in the collective spirit of a nation that strives for progress, justice, and a better future for all. Canada's Greatest of All Time are not just historical figures but an inspiration for all Canadians to continue shaping a brighter tomorrow. Their legacies live on, and their stories encourage us to reach new heights, break barriers, and leave our own positive mark on the world.

.....***.....

Printed in Great Britain
by Amazon

32980506R00040